Investing for Beginners

An Introduction to Easy and Successful Investing

By

Frank Elynbridge

Copyright © 2017 Frank Elynbridge
All rights reserved.
ISBN: 1544680171
ISBN-13: 978-1544680170

Table of Contents

Investing for Beginners _____ 1

Introduction _____ 4

Chapter 1: What Is Investing? _____ 7

Chapter 2: Investing Methods _____ 13

Chapter 3: Getting Started _____ 26

Chapter 4: Additional Investment Vehicles _____ 47

Chapter 5: Investment Properties _____ 54

Chapter 6: Mistakes to Avoid _____ 63

Chapter 7: The Golden Rules _____ 87

Conclusion _____ 110

Introduction

Thank you for purchasing *"Investing for Beginners:* An Introduction to Easy and Successful Investing". This book is intended to help everyday people like yourself understand the world of investing and learn how you can maximize your income through smart investments.

Unless you hold a college or university degree, the world of investments can be confusing and daunting. This book is intended to help you understand investments on a deeper level and make wise decisions that will multiply your income and make your money work for you!

If you have ever handled any kind of money in your life, as we all have, then you have likely heard a lot about investments. Just about everyone talks about investments in their lives, and for good reason. Investing wisely and appropriately based on your income levels and needs can multiply your money so that you end up earning more, simply by investing in the right areas! Once upon a time, investing your money was only for the wealthy and for those who had money to begin with. Nowadays, absolutely anyone can invest their money.

There are amazing people out there who can help you, and then there are ones who want to capitalize off of you. This book is going to give you a solid understanding of investments so that you can learn exactly what you need to do to invest your money, and so that you can ensure that any investor you are working with is working for your own good.

Investing is a wise and powerful way to grow your money with minimal effort and continue watching it grow. If you have ever dreamed of earning money while you sleep, or earning *more* money while you sleep, then you need to step bravely into the world of investing and see what your money really can do for you! If you are ready to learn all about the basics of investing and how you can take advantage of this simple way to grow your money, then read on! This book has been carefully written to ensure that you understand everything you are reading and that you feel confident making these decisions with your own money. Please enjoy!

Chapter 1: What Is Investing?

There are several different ways that you can invest money, as the options are nearly limitless. It can be hard for the average person to know where to begin, so we are going to take this slowly and carefully! That way, you will feel confident in knowing exactly where your money is going, how it is working for you, and why. The more knowledge you have going into your investment portfolio, the easier it will be to ensure that you are making money! In this chapter, we are going to discuss the basics.

What Is Investing?

Investing essentially means that you pay money into something that will earn you more money back. You are making your money work for you so that it multiplies without you even having to work for that growth. While many people believe the main way to earn income is by working, often they forget that you can actually earn an additional income through investing. When you invest in a smart way, you can increase your income exponentially. Investing is considered a form of passive income because you simply make a decision and then your money does the work for you. You can literally earn money in your sleep when you invest it properly. Investing is an incredibly smart opportunity to increase your wealth and earn more income. It is important that everyone learn the basics of investing and use it as an opportunity to make your money work for you, instead of you constantly having to work for their money!

What *Isn't* Investing?

Many people believe that investing is a dangerous game to play and that you are gambling off your money. The reality is that that is not what investing is like at all. Gambling means that you are putting a sum of money up for risk with virtually no guarantee that you will receive any kind of payoff. Your odds of earning money are often low, and if you do win, it's not common for you to be able to do it again and again.

When you invest your money wisely, as you will learn to do in this book, you can almost guarantee that you will gain money back. Of course, there are no solid guarantees, but for the most part, a well-calculated investment will *always* pay off. While there is a risk involved, it is a lot less risky than simply purchasing a lotto ticket and praying that it pays off. You are much more likely to have your investment pay off than you are to have a random gamble pay off!

Why Does Investing Work?

Investing works by putting your money towards something and having it earn money back. Most investments are a numbers game that is based on a percentage of interest. When you put money into an investment, you earn interest back on that money. While that interest will fluctuate from week to week and month to month, in the grand scheme of things it is will more than likely be on the up rise. That means after several months, your money will have grown significantly.

A major reason why people become fearful of investing is because of the amount that that percentage fluctuates. They fear that the risk of the number moving around will equate to them not earning anything, or worse, losing everything. The reality is, you would not lose everything. When you understand investments, you will know that over time they virtually always earn some level of money. The only way you are likely to lose a significant amount of money is if you take an uncalculated risk and invest your money with zero knowledge on what you are investing in. When you are investing wisely, though, you will have calculated your risk and you will know that you are going to earn money back.

Who Should Invest?

While investing used to be something done by only businessmen and those of wealth, investing has become a staple in the average individual's wealth portfolio. Whether you earn only a couple of thousand a year, or several million per year, investing is an important thing for you to do. Investing has become an incredible tool that enables virtually everyone to grow their wealth and earn an investment income.

Investing is a great way to save for and guarantee a retirement, education funds, and more. You can invest short term or long term, you can invest for a specific use, or simply to grow your wealth, or you can invest for any number of other reasons. Investing is a powerful opportunity to increase your earning potential and provide greater security for your future and your freedom.

Investing may seem intimidating and scary in the beginning, but once you understand it, it is really easy. Remember, if you are unaware of what you are doing yourself, you can always hire an investment portfolio manager. These individuals are powerful assistants in assuring that your money works for you. However, having a strong knowledge of the world of investment will ensure that you can do this yourself if you desire, or that you will be confident that your investment portfolio manager is working in your favor every single time.

Chapter 2: Investing Methods

At first, seeing all of the different terminology and styles of investing can be overwhelming. There are a lot! When you look deeper into it, though, there really are only a few ways. In this chapter, you are going to learn more about those ways and uncover which of them are important, and why. By the end of this chapter, you should have a clear understanding of what types of investment methods are available to you.

Bank Products

Virtually all banks and credit unions offer an opportunity for you to invest your money. These methods are usually the safest route to help you accumulate savings on your income. Some of the banks out there even offer you services that will assist you in managing your money and earning the most that you possibly can from it.

While these products tend to have a lower earning potential than other products, their earning potential is almost guaranteed. It is the lowest possible risk route for investors to go. There are three types of accounts you are likely to have with a bank: a savings account, a money market account, or a certificate deposit. Savings accounts are ones that have a fixed interest rate and allow you to earn on a regular basis. If you have enough money saved, many bank accounts offer high-interest savings accounts that allow you to earn even more. Money market accounts are similar to savings accounts, but often have a higher balance requirement than an average savings account would. These offer higher rates of interest for accounts with larger balances. Certificates of deposits are term deposits, which essentially means that you give the bank money and agree that you won't use it for a set amount of time. At the end of the term, you can liquidate the account or choose to add more and start a new term. These allow you to earn even more than other accounts and are still lower risk than other methods of investments.

Bonds

Bond investments allow an individual to invest money into a corporation, federal agency, government or otherwise in return for payments of interest over a specified time period. In addition to the interest payments, you will get the principle repaid to you at the end of the term, also known as the bond's maturity date. There are a number of bond types that you can invest in, ranging from government bonds to corporate bonds, international bonds and more. Bonds have a higher risk the longer you invest them, and the risk varies based on which bond you choose to invest in. These are a highly common investment route that people go. Assuming that you research the investment prior to making your move, you are likely to make your money back from this method.

Stocks

When people think of investing, stocks is one of the first things they think of. People either love stocks or hate stocks, they're rarely in between. Those who hate stocks are often ones who do not understand the stock market and don't realize the potential that it has.

Stocks are a part of the stock market. You invest in them by buying stocks, which means you buy a share of a company. The risk associated with stocks tends to be higher, especially if you enter your investment with minimal research. The surefire way to get your money back is to ensure that you invest in a company that is destined to succeed. If you invest in stock associated with a company that fails, then you will lose your money. That is why people think that investments are a gamble and that you are at risk to lose everything. If you invest without research and simply jump in feet first, there is a good chance you will lose money. However, if you invest wisely and do your research, the stock market shows a history of being on a constant uprise over a long period of time. That being said, the longer you are in the market, the greater your rate of return will be.

Investment Funds

There are two types of investment funds, and these are another popular investment method for average people. Funds are often associated with a lower-risk investment opportunity, and these are the ones that are often considered "a must" by the average person. They include mutual funds and exchange-traded funds.

Mutual funds are the most popular method and include investments such as RRSPs, RESPs, and other similar styles of investments. With mutual funds, several people get together and invest money with a common goal. Then, someone manages the account and plays the field to invest the money in the best possible way to earn money back. It may be invested in stocks, bonds, or other styles of investments. All who invested in the fund, then, will get a return back from the interest earned and the growth of the funds.

Exchange-traded funds are sort of a hybrid between mutual funds and conventional stock investments. Unlike mutual funds, exchange-traded funds are traded on the stock market. Similar to mutual funds, though, they have a series of investors involved that help to provide a diversified portfolio.

In general, these are the most popular styles of investments for average people. They are lower risk with a comfortable rate of return. While it doesn't have the potential to be as high as some other methods may be, it is still a powerful way to invest.

Annuities

An annuity is an investment you make in an insurance company, essentially. You and an insurance company will write up a contract and the insurance company will promise to pay you a certain amount starting either immediately or at some point in the future.

You can purchase an annuity in one lump sum, or you can pay premiums to purchase it over a period of time. Annuities can be used for several reasons, including retirement, or any other reason why you would want to stop working and earn an income from your savings instead. A "deferred annuity" represents an annuity that isn't scheduled to start until sometime in the future, and an "immediate annuity" is one that is scheduled to start immediately. There are two types of annuities you can invest in: fixed and variable. Fixed will provide you with a guaranteed rate of return, and variables will, as you may have guessed, have a varied rate. There are also indexed annuities which provide you a minimum rate of guaranteed interest and then have an additional part of the interest that fluctuates. In essence, an indexed annuity is the best of both worlds!

Saving for College or University

There are many ways to save for college and/or university. If you are looking to set aside an educational savings fund for someone, there are a few routes you can choose. For starters, you will want to estimate what your savings need to be in order to send said child to university in the future. Remember, rates rise each year, so it is important to plan for about 5% increase per year.

Include this in your savings estimate.

The four main opportunities for you to save for school include 529 college savings plans, 529 prepaid tuition plans, Coverdell's and custodial accounts, and savings bonds. A 529 college savings plan allows you to gain interest on your savings and prevents you from having to pay taxes in the future. A 529 prepaid tuition plan allows for you to prepay for someone's tuition at today's rate so that they do not have to pay the increased amount in the future. Coverdell's and custodial accounts do not allow you to save as much as the 529's, and they also don't earn as much in return. However, you do have your entire portfolio already managed for you without you having to do anything else. Finally, there are series EE savings accounts that you can use to save for college and prevent yourself or said person from having to pay taxes on that amount in the future.

Retirement

There are several opportunities to save for retirement which is important to note when you are preparing your investment portfolio. The earlier you start saving the better, as it will give you more money to retire with later. There are about four primary ways to invest your money to save for your retirement. The most common way in the United States is through a 401(k) investment. In Canada, these are similar to RRSPs. They allow you to save a set amount each month, provide you with tax benefits, and allow your savings to compound over time. Individual Retirement Accounts (IRAs) are an excellent way for you to set aside retirement savings as well and will pay you out on a monthly basis when you are ready to retire. Target-Date Funds, also known as life-cycle funds, are investments where you pick your target retirement date and the portfolio is managed to help you have enough savings to do so.

They are not risk-free, even once the target date has been reached, however. Finally, there are also smart automatic retirement plan investments. These are plans held by employers that require virtually nothing from you, the investments are done automatically through your employer.

Options

Simply put, options are contracts that give you (the purchaser) the right to buy or sell securities. These securities may be stocks or exchange-traded funds that you can buy or sell at a fixed priced for a specific set of time. With an option, you do have the right, but you do not have the obligation to buy or sell your securities.

Insurance

You can purchase insurances as a part of an overall financial plan. This insurance, in particular, refers to life insurance. There are a number of different models of life insurances that you can buy that protect your assets and debts for the future generation. When you pay into life insurance, you give your family the security of knowing that they won't owe money on your debts and that your assets will not be liquidated to pay the debts if they can't afford them. In essence, everything financially will continue to run along smoothly. You will also get a fixed amount of money paid out to your family to cover end of life expenses and have mourning money as well. The types of life insurance you can get include term life, whole life, universal life, variable life, and variable universal life. Each has a unique benefit to it that makes it work for your family.

There are many different types of investments that you should consider when you are looking to invest your money. Most people have an investment portfolio that covers a few different styles of investments. This gives them money now, in the near future, in the distant future, and money for their family after they pass away. Essentially when you invest your money you are paying for your future now. It may seem redundant, but when you arrive in your future self, you will realize how much less stress you have when you see that you are financially covered going forward.

After reading all of these different styles of investments, you are likely feeling a bit overwhelmed. This is completely normal. Remember that you don't need to invest in all of the aforementioned investment vehicles and that you don't need a lot of money to invest in order to make it worthwhile, either. In the remaining chapters of this book, you are going to learn how to build your investors portfolio and make your money work for your unique needs.

Chapter 3: Getting Started

There is a certain process to getting started when you are preparing to invest your money. When you are getting started, you will want to take your time and do all of the groundwork so that you know you are doing the right thing for you and your needs. Whether you are an individual, a family, a non-profit or otherwise, you are going to want to make sure that you take the time to get the basics together so that you can ensure all of your needs are met through your investment decisions.

An Investor's Portfolio

Before you begin investing, you are going to need to create your portfolio. Your portfolio assesses several major elements of your investing needs and desires to ensure that your money is working properly for you.

Since there are many ways you can invest and many reasons why you would want to invest, it is important that you thoroughly address your portfolio first, to ensure you are investing in all of the right ways for all of the right reasons. You investing portfolio covers several major areas, which we will discuss in further detail now.

Numbers You Should Know

There are four major numbers you need to know. These numbers are important to help you understand what your investment needs are and why you are intending on investing your money. By knowing this, you will later be able to find out what you should invest in and how. The numbers you need to know include:

1. What You Own: all of your assets, savings, and existing investments. You should consider the valuation of your assets, and write them down in monetary value. (Your assets include your home, cars, and other large ticket items like boats, etc.)
2. What You Owe: all of your outstanding debts need to be added up.
3. What You Earn: your total income value. (Including your salary, investment income, and anywhere else you earn income in your life.)
4. What You Spend: track every dollar you spend every month and write this down.

You want to get exact numbers on these, or as close to being exact as possible. The more exact you are on these, the better your knowledge on your own investment style and needs. This will help ensure you are making the right move with your money when you are preparing to invest it.

You should write these numbers down on a spreadsheet, and keep them handy.

Your Financial Goals

Now that you see your financial situation, you are ready to set up your financial goals. You will want to be very specific about what your goals are. You should have a dollar value available, and a timeframe in which you want to achieve said goal. Consider all of your financial goals for the future and include them here. If you are unsure about how your goals should look, here are five examples of clear and effective financial goals:

1. Save $50,000 for a down payment on a house in the next year.
2. Pay off remaining credit card balance in the next 3 months.
3. Save $40,000 for child's education by the time she graduates at 18.
4. Have 6 months worth of living expenses saved up within' 1 year.
5. Pay off $29,000 car loan in the next 4 years.

You need to be specific, realistic and clear on what your goals are. The more focused you are, the easier it will be to set up a focused plan so that you achieve them. You will use your financial situation and your financial goals to create your financial plan, including what you want to invest in and how.

Your Unique Investing Personality

There are a few different investing personalities that you may be. They range from conservative-risk to high-risk. Most people have a few different personalities, depending on the specific investment at hand. For example, you may be conservative with your retirement savings, but high-risk with just a general investment you are doing to earn extra investment income. There are a few ways to identify what your investment personality is, but in general, you will find out based on what feels right to you for each individual investment.

There are four particular questions you need to ask yourself when making an investment. You should ask yourself these questions about every single investment you make. Like previously stated, your personality will likely change depending on what the investment is itself.

1. How much risk can I tolerate on this investment?

Your risk tolerance will identify whether you are a conservative- or high-risk investor for this particular investment. Conservative investments are one where you don't take as big of a risk and your potential rate of return is lower but more guaranteed. High risk means that your potential rate of return is higher, but your risk of losing is also greater. You should identify how much you are willing to lose and what you're comfortable with risking. Generally, with money you will rely on more, you are going to want to choose a conservative or moderate risk investment. With something that is just extra income or something that you won't end up relying on, you may wish to go moderate or even high risk on your investment.

2. How much do I expect to make from my investments?

If you want to make a lot of money back, you are going to go with your highest comfortable risk. If you are comfortable with enduring that risk for a greater return, then it may be a good idea to go higher risk. However, if you want to make a consistent return and are not concerned about making a large amount back, or if you want a more secure investment, then you are going to want to go with lower risk.

3. How long do I want to invest for?

The amount of time you want to invest for should also come into play when you are deciding what you want to invest as. If you are choosing a shorter term investment, you are likely going to want to pick a conservative or moderate risk investment so that you have a more guaranteed return. However, if you have a longer time to produce your money, you may want to choose a higher risk investment and then adjust it when the term is coming closer to its end. This way, you have more of an opportunity to make a greater return, but you can adjust it to a conservative risk as you get closer to the investment's maturity to ensure that you don't take a last minute hit on your investment.

4. How quickly do I need to access my money?

When you want to access your money is important. If you want to access it right away, you are almost definitely going to be investing at a conservative risk. However, if you will definitely not need access right away, you may wish to choose something with a greater return potential that will also carry a higher risk.

Ultimately, you are going to want to clearly answer these questions, gain an idea of what suits you best, and then consider what you feel most comfortable with doing. You are not going to be forced in at any investment level. You need to honestly and realistically consider your needs and choose investments that will match those needs. If you are not someone who is willing to risk a large amount to potentially make a large amount, then you should never feel pressured to invest in a high-risk portfolio. If you are more interested in a conservative, conservative-moderate or moderate investment portfolio, then go this route. While you may not make as much back, your money will still be working for you and you will still make a steady amount back.

Understanding Your Risk Tolerance
In the previous section, you learned about your portfolio personality. Now, you are going to

learn more about risk tolerance so you can be very clear on where you truly fall.

Just because the idea of higher gains seems rewarding doesn't always mean it is the best risk for you to take. There are many things you need to consider when you are deciding on your risk tolerance. The following are things you should consider:

- A higher risk means a higher chance of reward, but it does not guarantee it
- There are different types of investment risk from market risk to equity risk and more, you should investigate which kinds you are subject to with different investments and consider these
- Diversification allows you to reduce risk by having your money invested in many areas, but this is only valuable if you have enough money to do so (mutual funds are a great way to get a diversified portfolio if you don't have a lot of funds, for example)

- If you need to liquidate soon, you don't want to run a high risk
- If you can hold off and know you won't need the money anytime soon, it might be a better idea to go higher risk
- Inflation risk means that if you do not have a good enough rate of return, your purchasing power may not be protected

There are many things you want to truly consider when you are determining what your risk factor is. Many of us do not want to risk losing money because we work hard for it and it can be hard to replenish that money if we lose it. However, there may be certain instances where you are willing to have a higher risk because the potential return is higher.

When you are investing, it is a good idea to have some money invested in various risk levels. This helps guarantee that you won't lose everything should something go wrong. As well, the higher the risk associated with your investment, the more closely you will want to pay attention to it to ensure that you are making smart choices with it. This is where an investment portfolio manager comes in handy, as they are trained to help manage this for you.

Create Your Final Plan
No plan is ever completely final, but at this time you are going to want to create your finalized plan which is the one you will follow for the time being. By now, you should have specific and realistic goals set in place. You may wish to tweak these goals based on what you now know about your risk tolerances and such.

So, make sure that you have created realistic goals that you want to reach, and have the timeline of when you want to reach them in place. Remember, your goals need to be specific so you know exactly what you are working towards.

Now that you know what your goals are, you should calculate how much you need to save each month to meet these goals. So, let's say you want to have $25,000 saved up for a house by the end of the year, and there are 9 months left in the year. Given that information, you know that you will need to save about $2775 every month in order to have that. You should do this with all of your plans so that you have the amount you will need to save each month for each goal. Then, you can add these savings together. So, let's say you need $2775 per month towards your house, $325 per month towards your child's education fund, and $200 per month towards your credit card debt. Your total savings would then need to be $3300 per month in order to reach your goals.

Now that you know what you need to save and how long you have to save for, you can decide what type of investment you want to do. For longer term goals, you may want to choose investments that are more aggressive and carry a higher risk which would give you the greatest chance of reaching or exceeding those goals. For shorter term goals, you are going to want to choose something between conservative or moderate and ensure that you are in a lower-risk category so that you can be sure that the money will be there when you need it.

You need to create an investment policy statement that is going to help you guide your investment decisions. If you are working with a portfolio manager or an adviser, you are going to have one of these made for you with or by the adviser. The investment policy needs to include:
- A clear statement of your goals and your objectives
- The strategies that you will use to help you meet your goals and objectives

- When your return expectations are and the time horizon you have
- A detailed account of your risk tolerance overall, as well as your risk tolerance per specified area
- A guideline that details the types of investments that will make up your portfolio, as well as how accessible you need your money to be, and
- How exactly your portfolio will be monitored and managed and when or why it should be rebalanced in the future (for example, a goal is met so you want to reinvest that money elsewhere)

Choosing Your Asset Mix

You want to have a well-diversified portfolio, so you are going to need to choose an asset mix that helps ensure you get this. If you are working with an adviser you will have some involvement in this process but you will have guidance on it. If you are investing alone, however, you are going to need to take extra time to consider what you are investing in and how it contributes to your portfolio.

A well-diversified portfolio means that you have your money invested in a few ways to ensure that you have your money working for you to the best of its ability, and to protect you from extreme losses. There are three main areas that your portfolio should be invested in: cash and cash equivalents, fixed income investments and equities. When you decide where you are going to invest your money this way, it is called asset allocation. Essentially you are deciding where you will allocate your money into.

When you are choosing your asset mix, it should:
- Ensure that your risk and expected rate of return are balanced
- Fit your risk tolerance
- Allow you to get your money at the time that you will need it

- Provide you with the growth you need in order to reach your goals, and
- Evolve with you as your needs evolve

The last point is important: as you change through the stages of your life, your investment needs and personality are going to change, as well. For example, if you are new and in your first job, you are likely going to have a more conservative investment personality because you don't want to lose your savings since you likely don't have a savings to begin with. However, when you are more established in your career you will likely have more money to play with and will want to potentially change to a more aggressive investment personality. Finally, when you are coming closer to your retirement, you are going to want to shift gears and head back into a more conservative and lower-risk investment personality type to ensure that you have a healthy number of funds to retire with. It is natural and normal for your investment personality to evolve over time, even several times over.

Ensure that you allow room for this when you are preparing your asset allocation plan.

Managing Your Investment
It is important that you continue to manage your investments after you have made them, even if you have an advisor managing your portfolio. Having regular checkups allows you to ensure that your money is working for you, to make any necessary changes you may want or need to have made, and otherwise make sure that everything is working in your favor. There are three primary reasons why you want to ensure that you are managing your account, and how you should be doing it:

1. See how your investments are performing
   You can and should check your statements as they come in to ensure that your investments are growing and returning at a rate which you desire. If you have any

questions about how your money is working for you, you should speak with your advisor to help have these questions answered. If you are managing it yourself, watching these numbers will help you decide what to do and when.

2. Know what you are paying in fees

You often pay some level of fees on your investments, so it is important to watch what fees you are paying. Your statements will tell you more about this. If you feel you are paying too much for your investments, you may want to look into alternative and more affordable options.

3. Make any necessary adjustments

Monitoring your investments allows you to know when your needs have evolved and at what time you need to adjust to suit these needs. Or, sometimes your needs don't change but you realize there are ways that your income could be expanding better if your portfolio were altered slightly. Monitoring your investments helps you know what to do and when.

Putting It All Together

All of the aforementioned information is involved in creating a powerful investment portfolio that will address your needs and concerns and ensure that you are getting the best possible return on your money. When you are creating your portfolio, it is important that you are realistic, or even conservatively realistic. Money is an important commodity that we need to monitor and maintain to ensure that it is always working for us. Investing is a great way to ensure that your money is working hard for you.

If you are comfortable with managing your own investment portfolio, you can do so.

However, if you are unsure about investments, it is a good idea to get an advisor. Still, it is powerful to have a basic knowledge about investments before you hire an advisor so that you can weigh in your knowledge and concerns, and so that you can be sure that your advisor has your best interest in mind. This way, you can be sure that your money is protected and working hard for you.

Chapter 4: Additional Investment Vehicles

In addition to working with an investment portfolio that includes stocks, bonds, mutual funds and the likes, there are other formats of investments that you may wish to consider. In this section, you are going to look into alternative investment opportunities and how they can work for you. You may wish to use one of these in addition to or as an alternative to the aforementioned investment styles. If you do, you are still going to want to take the time to create your investment portfolio to ensure that you are choosing investment vehicles that will properly serve your needs.

Directly Investing in Private Companies and Start-Ups

When you are looking to invest your money, you may wish to invest directly into a specific private company or company start up. This strategy carries a high risk but also carries a high reward potential. If you invest in a company that fails, you may not receive any of your money back. However, if you invest in a company that takes off and succeeds really well, then you are likely to make a major return on your investment. Generally speaking, you don't want to invest in companies unless you have a good idea of what will make a company succeed and how you can ensure that you are investing in an idea that is going to help you earn back your principle and then some.

If you do not wish to put the high risk into a start-up, you may wish to instead invest into a company that is already mature. Most companies require investments many times throughout their life cycles, which means that there will be many opportunities to invest in their stock. When you are investing in a company, the more mature and successful said company is, the more expensive it will become to invest in it. This is generally a good sign, however, as it shows that said company has been excelling and that they have a strong potential to help you return your investment.

In some places, you have to have a minimum number of assets or capital in order to invest in companies like this. For example, "angel investors" are investors who invest in start-ups and help them raise the capital they need to launch their business. To become an angel investor, you need at least $1 million to your name to ensure that you will be able to invest without running yourself bankrupt. Before investing in a company this way, you will want to ensure that there are no laws or rules that state that you cannot invest in said company for any reason.

Real Assets

When you invest in real assets, you are investing in tangible items that have the ability to hold your money or increase your value. These investments are things that you purchase now and then you can sell them later to gain back money. Or, you simply hold on to these items and your asset value increases over time.

There are many items that fall into this category that are valid methods of investing. They include:
- Real estate and investment properties
- Oil
- Commodities such as precious metal
- Agricultural land

- Luxury and collectible items (i.e., art, jewelry, wine, rare items, and more)

It is not always possible to ensure that an investment in a real asset is going to pay off in the long run. However, sometimes you can be sure that an item will grow in value. For example, real estate almost always returns your investment or increases the return on your investment, especially the longer you hold onto it. It is common for real asset investment to be involved in people's portfolios.

Hedge Funds

Hedge funds include pooled investments by multiple people that are then used to invest in a variety of investments to help each investor gain capital. There are a few common styles of hedge fund strategies that are used to help raise funds for those who invest. They include equity long-short, arbitrage, distressed assets and macro-trends. Unlike private equity and venture capital, these investments are invested in public equities and often have a greater redemption frequency and liquidity. This means that those who invest in hedge funds can get their money out more frequently without paying a fine or fee to get it.

Investing in these alternative methods is a great way to further diversify your portfolio and increase your potential to receive a great return back. You want to make sure that when you are investing, you are always being careful.

Since these investment opportunities generally don't have a portfolio manager or advisor helping you out, you want to make sure that you are well educated on what you are investing your money into and that you have a high chance of making your money back. That way, you can be sure that your money will work for you and you will have a really good potential for getting a large amount of money back. In the next chapter, we are going to explore investment properties all on their own, as these investments are significantly different from other investment vehicles, but also have a high potential for earning you a great rate of return.

Chapter 5: Investment Properties

Investment properties are an incredible way to invest your money and make it back in several ways. While it is not like stocks, mutual funds or bonds, it is still a powerful way to invest your money into a real asset and make a great return back. In this chapter, you are going to learn more about what investment properties are and what they can do for you in regards to making an extra income!

Rental Properties

When you think about investing in real estate, you are likely thinking about rental properties. This means that you purchase a piece of real estate and you rent it out to tenants. In the beginning, your tenants may just pay the mortgage rate on the house.

However, once the mortgage has been paid for, you will be earning that monthly amount in profit. In this circumstance, you are responsible for paying for the mortgage, land taxes and property maintenance. You will want to make sure that the rent will cover all of these fees.

It is important that when you are searching for a rental property that you are purchasing a piece of property that is going to be able to return your investment. You should make sure it is in a place where you can comfortably charge what you want for rent, and where you will have your asset protected. With a rental property, you can manage the property yourself or you can hire a property manager to oversee the day to day parts of the investment and ensure that everything is looked after. When you have a property manager, you pay their wage plus the mortgage, maintenance, and property taxes. However, they are responsible for ensuring that everything is being looked after and that rent is collected every month.

Trading Real Estate

Another way to make money back on real estate is to purchase properties and flip them. This means that you buy a house that needs work for a nominal price, then you sell the house for a higher price and do it again and again. There are a couple of ways to do this.

The first style of property flipper is a person who purchases properties at low fees and instantly sells them. These people do not put any work into fixing them up or doing anything to them.

They simply buy them for a good price and sell them for a higher one. This is a good quick way to flip a market but it can become devastating if you cannot unload a property. You may end up having to pay a mortgage on a house that you aren't actively using which can become costly and will cost you more and more while you wait for someone to purchase it. If you are going to flip houses this way, you want to make sure the market is turning over fast so that you are able to earn a quick return.

The second style of property flipping is when you purchase a house that needs fixing and do all of the renovation work to it. You essentially give the house a face lift. Then, you sell the house for a higher price. This gives you the opportunity to make a much higher return on the property but will cost you a large initial investment and takes a lot longer than pure and simple house flipping. This strategy has been popularized by mainstream television and has become more common in the everyday housing market. If you have the time, energy and initial investment, it can be a great way to earn your money back and then some.

Investment Groups for Real Estate
Think of a mutual fund, only with real estate. That is what an investment group with real estate is. These individuals basically pool their resources together and buy into an investment property.

They may purchase a rental property, or they may purchase into house-flipping opportunities where they make fast cash back quick. When you do this, you often have the opportunity to invest in larger properties and make larger returns.

Usually, it works by having a single company build an apartment building or other multi-space complexes and then several investors go in on the property together. You may have a set investment group or you may buy into one when you purchase a percentage of the land and others purchase a percentage as well. At this time, you will all own a part of this building development and will make money off of it together. Investment groups are often offered by companies, so you can buy in and enter a relatively low-risk real estate investment. These companies use some of the money to pool it together so that if there are occasional vacancies in the building no one ends up suffering the losses.

Real Estate Limited Partnerships

When you are buying into real estate, you may prefer to go with a Real Estate Limited Partnership. This is a group of people who agree to enter a partnership for a finite amount of time and invest in properties. They may invest in many, or they may only invest in one. They pool their resources, invest in these properties, and split the returns on it. The group will form and then outside investors get together under a limited partnership to help finance the building itself. The real payoff with these buildings comes after the property has sold. Properties generally increase in value over time, so if the group holds the property for a decade or two, they will end up likely having a major return from said property.

REITs

Also known as a Real Estate Investment Trust, this is something that corporations (or trusts) do in order to capitalize on the real estate industry. They essentially purchase, operate and then sell income properties and anyone who buys into the trust makes money back. This business is designed so that 90% of the taxable profits must be paid out in the form of dividends. This eliminates the need for this business type to have to pay corporate income tax so that the tax doesn't eat into the income that is distributed to the shareholders.

Real Estate Mutual Funds

When you invest in real estate mutual funds, you are primarily investing in REITs and other real estate operating companies. These opportunities give you the ability to further diversify your portfolio and increase your earning potential and rate of return on your investments. These funds are fairly liquid, so you can get into them relatively easily and won't have to worry about the long-term investment that would otherwise come with investing in a large real estate property.

Investing in real estate is a great way to invest your money and get a great return. With real estate, you will almost always gain your return back. In general, real estate goes on an up rise in valuation. So, if you wait long enough you can always make your money back. The only drawback with real estate is that if you want to liquidate you may not make a significant amount back, and you may not be able to sell at a reasonable price or even right away. When the market is in a recession, it can be hard to offload a house. Still, if you have the time to wait, you can generally get into it and make a great return back.

One valuable thing about real estate investments that is worth noting is that these days, real estate investments are easier than ever for everyone to get involved in. While you may want to have more money to get into the type of real estate you desire, you can still get involved through real estate mutual funds or shorter-term investments that can be easily liquidated.

This is a great opportunity for the average layman to get their hands into real estate and make some money as a result. The housing market is a powerful investment strategy!

Chapter 6: Mistakes to Avoid

When you are investing, there are some mistakes you are going to want to avoid. These mistakes are fairly common, especially for beginners, and they can be very costly. It is best to educate yourself on these before you get started with investing, to ensure that you don't make any of them and that you save as much of your money, time and effort as possible. This chapter is going to outline the most common mistakes that are made in the investment industry and how you can avoid them.

Expecting Too Much

Investments alone are not enough to provide you with an income or solve all of your financial problems. While they are a great asset to add to your income streams, they should never be relied on as the only asset.

You should realize that your investments are a powerful way to transform your income and your financial situation, but they will not solve every problem. You still need to be working with your money in other ways to prepare for the present and the future, to ensure that you are prepared no matter what.

Using Someone Else's Expectations

In addition to not setting your own expectations too high, you should not rely on someone else's expectations, either. Just because someone made a lot off of investments doesn't guarantee that you will. It doesn't even guarantee that their advice will help ensure that you do. It is important that you set your own expectations and that you set them realistically so that you are earning what you intend to earn. You are not likely to become filthy rich off of investments. However, they are a great way to add to your overall financial plan.

It is important to note that even an advisor should be questioned. Many times advisors will offer a promising situation, assuring you that you will make tons of money back and that it will make you rich or help completely change your money game. The reality is, investments are investments. There is always a chance that you could make a lot, but generally, the return is more steady and smaller. Don't let an advisor or anyone else lead you to believe that you will get filthy rich doing this.

Not Having Clear Goals

If you don't have clear goals, it will be hard to meet them. This is true with anything in life, but especially with investments. It is important to make sure that you go into your investment situation knowing exactly what you want and what you are looking for. For many people this isn't an issue, the primary savings is generally retirement and that can be easy enough. However, if you are adding more goals in there, such as to save for your child's education or to save for a house, you need to be clear and specific on what you want. How much do you want to save, and what is your deadline? You need to be precise and exact to ensure that you make all of the best decisions to help you get to that level. Again, your goals should be realistic. If you are earning $20,000 a year and want to have $60,000 saved by the end of the year to buy a house, it probably won't happen. However, if you want to save $60,000 in 5 years, that would be a more realistic and clear goal. Using your investments wisely can help you achieve this goal, too. The more clear and realistic you are, the easier it will be to ensure that you actually reach your goals.

Failing to Diversify Enough

The purpose of diversifying your portfolio is to maximize your gains. It is to prevent you from, as they say, "putting all of your eggs in one basket". When you diversify your portfolio, you invest a certain amount into various areas. This ensures that if one area falls flat, your entire investment won't be affected by it. It keeps you from losing large amounts of money. You should make sure that your portfolio is diversified across several different investments. So, while you can diversify by buying into different stocks or mutual funds, you should also diversify by buying into different types of investments. Mutual funds, bonds, stocks, exchange-traded funds, and more should all be focused on. If anything goes wrong, you will end up still having other investment opportunities to rely on.

Buy High and Sell Low

Something that is common with new investors is buying high and selling low. When you do this, you are pretty much guaranteed to lose money. If you are buying after the stock has done really well, then you are buying too high. It is a good idea to wait until the stocks go low and purchase then so that you are not wasting your money spending more than you have to. Then, when the stocks are doing really well, you sell them. You want to buy low and sell high, not the other way around.

Many people panic when the stocks aren't doing well and they think that they need to jump ship and sell. The reality is, this loses you a lot of money and destroys your opportunity to gain more. This is exactly when you should be purchasing more stocks - when everyone else is panicking and selling. Then, when the stocks go up and *other* people are thinking "oh, now's the time to get in!" you wait until the market gets really hot and then sell them off. When you buy high and sell low, you destroy your "profit margin" and waste any chance you have at making a good return on your investment. Having a portfolio manager helps you reduce your risk of doing this, but if you are doing it all yourself, be sure that you keep this in mind.

Trading Too Much, Too Often

When you purchase any type of investment, you want to let it sit for some time so that it can do its work for you. If you trade too much or you trade too often, you obliterate any chance it has at earning you any money. Most stocks earn interest over time, so you need to let them sit for several months, sometimes even several years to get a really impactful gain from them.

Many people make the mistake of seeing the greener grass on the other side of the fence and they basically rob themselves of any chance they have of earning a good return. If you are going to commit to an investment, let it sit for a while. This is even true with stocks. While you are going to want to trade your stocks fairly regularly, you don't want to be trading them too fast. This just equals more work for less return!

Paying High Fees and Commissions

There are always fees and commissions associated with different brokerages, but you will want to make sure that you're paying attention to how much you are paying for your fees. You need to make sure that you aren't paying too much in fees and commissions because this results in much less being actually invested into you and your own planner.

There are two things you can do to prevent having to pay these fees and commissions, or at least prevent having to pay high fees and commissions. If you really want an advisor, you should shop around and make sure that you are getting one who suits your needs, but who also doesn't charge too much for you to work with them. Or, to avoid the fees and commissions altogether, you can simply learn how to manage your own investment portfolio and invest yourself. This bypasses the middle man and saves you a large amount of money. It is not too hard to do, but if you are not someone who is overly aware of what to do, it may be best to start out with an advisor. Then, once you get the swing of things, you could consider going off on your own.

Too Much Focus on Taxes

Many people put a significant amount of focus onto the tax consequences onto their investment options and fail to look at the overall gains they are facing when they are making their investments. Making moves that minimize the amount of taxes you have to pay is a smart move, but not when it is to the detriment of your own return. Often, the taxes you pay are minimal compared to what you would be earning in return. If you are focusing too heavily on the taxes associated with your investments, then you are likely doing yourself a disservice. Make sure that you look at the bigger picture, and not just your returns. This way, you can ensure that you are making enough money in return and that you are not robbing yourself of the opportunity of greater gains due to the fear of a greater tax margin.

Not Enough Reviewing of Investments

Something many people fail to do is regularly review your investments. Remember in a previous chapter when we spoke about managing your investments by regularly reviewing the statements? It is important for a reason. You need to make sure that you are always keeping an eye on your investments and that they are working well for you. While you don't want to invest too much or too often, it is important that you make sure that your money is working in your favor. This can take some adjustments in the beginning sometimes, to ensure that it is doing the best it can for you.

Additionally, your needs or situation may change more frequently than you realize. If you fail to review your statements and performance on a regular basis, you may end up costing yourself a lot of money or losing yourself several opportunities to maximize your rate of return on your investments.

Taking the Wrong Risks

Many people struggle to find where they should take the right risks. They either take too much of a risk, too little of a risk, or they take the wrong risk, or maybe just at the wrong time. There is a lot that goes into making sure that you are taking the right risks and that you are not suffering from your decisions. It may seem intimidating to get the risk wrong, but if you pay attention to the questions and considerations made available to you earlier in this book, then you can get a better idea on how you should take a risk when you are investing.

In general, if the money isn't highly important to you and is maybe just extra funds, or if you won't need it right away and you have plenty of time to save it, you can generally get away with a higher risk portfolio. However, if you need the funds soon or at any given time, or if it is an extremely important investment to you (i.e. retirement or education) you will likely want to keep your investment risk on the lower and more conservative side. People who are younger and have plenty of time before their retirement often have a better chance at having a higher risk portfolio for a while before reducing to a more conservative portfolio in the long run. This is because they have a chance to earn back that money if they lose it, either through work or through waiting for the portfolio to go on the uptrend again. However, if you are closer to your retirement, you likely won't want to have a large risk associated with that fund as you are going to want to liquidate it soon.

Not Knowing the True Performance of Your Investments

Just because one investment is thriving doesn't mean they all are. It is important to make sure that all of your investments are working to your benefit. Your entire portfolio isn't based on your best investment any more than your entire life is based on one decision. You need to make sure that you are monitoring your entire portfolio and that you are clear on the true performance of *all* of your investments, not just one or two. This way, you can be sure that overall your investment portfolio is working for your highest benefit and that you are going to be able to get more money back as a result.

Media Reactions

You should absolutely never ever listen to the

media, ever. Many people listen to the media when they talk about how the stock has completely "tanked" or if it is "at an all-time high". The media is famous for exaggerating things to get people to listen, and if you make *any* decisions based solely off of what you heard through the media, you are doing yourself and your investments a major disservice. Do yourself a favor and tune out anything you hear on the media. If you are really, truly concerned, you can contact your advisor to make sure. However, the best way to ensure that your investments are still safe is to watch your own and how they are performing. If they are barely dipping and the media is calling an all-out halt of the stocks, you are probably seeing the extent of the dip. Or, it may dip a bit further. Still, remember that stocks always come back up, so just wait it out and let it come back. It is absolutely rare for an investment to truly tank as bad as the media will lead you to believe it will. For the sake of your investment portfolio and your money, just tune out anything to do with stock markets and investment information when it comes to the media. Your guide should be your performance reviews and your advisor, if you have one, only. Everything else is irrelevant.

Chasing Yields

There is zero point to chase yields. Just because a certain fund is doing better right now doesn't mean it will be doing better long-term. You need to make sure that you don't shop around from yield to yield and ruin your rate of return as a result. Remember, if it is holding a higher yield, it is also holding a higher yield. Jumping over will cost you a transaction fee, as well as running a higher risk of losing everything. Remember, you don't want to trade too much, too often. If you jump around like this, you run a higher risk of losing your investment, and you pay high amounts to do so. It completely takes away from your investment purposes and destroys your opportunity to earn money. The best thing you can do is stay confident in your position, knowing that you (or your portfolio manager) made a strong and educated decision in the move you (or they) made.

Trying to Be a Genius

Don't try to be a market-timing genius. Just don't. You will never be able to know exactly when a market is going to peak or fall. It varies so much that you will never be able to accurately know exactly what is happening and when. You are best to trade your investments with automated regularity and not move your investments around too much. Give your investments time to do work for you before you move them around. That way you maximize your earning potential and gains and minimize the amount of work and fees you invest in making changes that ultimately deviate away from your main goal.

Wrong Advisor

If you are working with an advisor, you have to realize that they are not all the same. You will not get the same service from one to the next. You are must realize that there are good investors and bad investors out there. Good investors are ones who can clearly understand your needs, honor them, and earn you as much as possible to help serve these needs. Bad ones will not listen, will not clearly understand what you need, may be pushy about what they think you need, will provide empty promises, and will not invest in a way that serves your highest earning potential. It is important that you take the time to research who you are getting as an advisor and that you are prepared to shop around a bit before settling down. You *can* interview advisors to find the one that fits you best. Then, when you do find one, you can stick with them. If you are unhappy with your advisor or you feel that they are not serving your needs the way that they should be, then you should move on and find a new one. When it comes to working with your money, it is important that the person doing it is working for your highest good.

Using Emotional Judgment

Many people make the terrible mistake of letting their judgment get clouded by emotions. If you make investment decisions based on your emotions, you are bound to lose money. These emotions often arise as a fear of the future. If you make any of your financial decisions based on emotions, then you are likely doing yourself a disservice in the long run. It is important that you are thinking with a clear mind and that you make logical and rational decisions when it comes to your finances. You should not ever make a decision based out of fear, anger, sadness, or even happiness. If you are overbound with emotions, you are likely to make a decision that does not clearly and accurately reflect your needs or desires. Doing this can result in major and costly mistakes that can, in worst case scenarios, ruin your investment portfolio. You should always work with a clear mind with as little emotional involvement as possible.

Forgetting About Inflation

Prices continue to rise and if you don't prepare for or plan for these rises, you may make improper investment decisions. Something that is often talked about in the investment world is "purchasing power". Purchasing power means that your money value is protected. So, let's say that today you could purchase a pack of gum for $1. You put that $1 in a regular savings account and in ten years you take it out. Only, now gum costs $1.50 so you can no longer buy gum with it. Really, you can't buy anything with it anymore, it is simply not enough. However, if you are accounting for inflation in your investments, you will protect your purchasing power. So, when gum rises to $1.50, your $1 will also increase to $1.50 in savings. In this case, you have protected your purchasing power. It is important that you think about and pay attention to your purchasing power and that you always account for inflation. This will protect you from making any decisions that negatively impact your money or leave you with not enough in the future.

A good way to think about it is: just because $100,000 may be enough to retire in today's world doesn't mean it will be enough for you to retire when the time actually comes. Therefore, you need to account for the inflation of costs and ensure that you save enough money to comfortably be able to retire when you are ready to. If you invest in the right portfolios, you will be protecting your purchasing power and saving yourself from the cost of inflation. When the time comes, your $100,000 will be equivalent to whatever the new required cost to retire is at that time.

Not Starting or Continuing

A shockingly high number of people become intimidated by investing and so they decide that they would rather not. As a result, they end up selling themselves short and they miss out on a great opportunity to increase their income. A retirement at the very least is something that you should be investing into. If you are not, then you are basically robbing your future self of financial freedom. Just because investing seems difficult doesn't mean that it has to be. If you are fearful of starting yourself, take the time to hire a professional and personable investment advisor and spend time letting them help you build your portfolio and make decisions that will work in your favor. This book is an excellent opportunity for you to develop a basic understanding and then you can either go forward to invest on your own, or hire an advisor that you *know* will be able to help you earn a significant amount of money.

Other people make the mistake of starting their investments but not continuing them. So, they put a significant amount in to start, but they stop investing on a regular basis or contributing at all. They don't manage their investment or review it, and over time they no longer have any idea what their money is doing for them. If you are doing this, you are also doing yourself a great disservice. It is important that you stay on track with your financial plan and that you continue to invest. If you have stopped because the plan has become too expensive or does not fit your needs or abilities anymore, then that typically means it's time to review it and make necessary changes so that your portfolio suits you better and is easier for you to maintain.

Not Controlling What is Within' Your Control

While you can't personally control a large amount of your investment portfolio, there are many things that you can control and you should take the time to understand what they are and then control them. For example, you can choose to spend less money on unnecessary items and then invest more into your future so that you are protected in the future. It is important to realize that when you are investing your money, it isn't going away. It is being set aside for *your* future and it is working to ensure that you have enough to retire with, or send your kids to school with, or do whatever else you have allotted that money for. Make sure that you are always taking advantage of what is in your control and that you are also working for your highest good with your money. That way, you can be sure that you are going to achieve all of your financial goals and that you will be well off!

There are many mistakes that people make when it comes to getting started with investing. Sometimes, their biggest mistake is that they don't even get started! There are many reasons why investing can be hard or intimidating, but if you educate yourself on what to do and then what *not* to do you, you give yourself the best opportunity to make sure that you are always going to have enough money for your and your family's future. As difficult or pointless as it may seem now, it is really important that you pay attention to your future. Doing this now will prevent you from having to do a significant amount of hard work later. The best way to claim financial freedom is to take advantage of your finances in the present and ensure that they are working for your highest benefit. It is never too soon or too late to start focusing on your investments and making sure that they are serving you and your needs.

Chapter 7: The Golden Rules

There are always rules that come in to play whenever you are doing something, especially when you are preparing to invest your hard earned money. When you are investing, you need to make sure that you focus on these rules to ensure that you maximize your investments and gain the best potential return from them possible. These rules are ones that have been picked from some of the best investors and, if you follow them, you should find that your investments work for your highest benefit.

Invest for Your Long Term Goals

An important part of investing is to ensure that you are investing for your long-term goals. When you do this, you ensure that you are focusing on your future and that you are giving yourself the highest opportunity to earn back your principle investment and then some. When you are investing, you are rarely putting aside money for the short term. In general, you are investing with the intention of saving or growing your funds for at least one year from today, and as far as several decades into the future. The more you focus on the long-term in your investments, the better you are going to be able to make your money work for you.

Investments are a means to save money through interest. That being said, you need to actually let your money sit in one place for long enough to gain interest. If you are only investing for a few weeks or months at a time, there is almost no point in investing it. You are going to end up wasting your money, as you will not have enough time to accrue any type of return on your investments. Most investments are made for the long-term. The shortest term you want to consider investing in is one year, but preferably 15 months or longer. By doing this, you give yourself the best chance of earning a strong rate of return.

When you are investing, you want to be investing for things such as education, retirement, unexpected illnesscs, or periods where you are without work unexpectedly. Otherwise, you should be putting your money aside in a simple savings account, or even a high-interest savings account. This will give you the best potential to earn money on your shorter term investments. Many people don't realize that if you invest in long-term investments but remove your money after a short period of time, you will actually pay higher fees and commissions on that money and it will end up costing you more.

It is a good idea to sit down and really consider what your long term goals are. What amount do you need to retire with? Do you have any kids you want to send to school? Are you going to invest in life insurance to make sure that your family is protected from your debts? What types of long-term investments are going to help you reach your long-term financial goals? It may seem difficult to really get all of this down at first, but the more you spend time on this, the better your long-term investment plan is going to be and the easier it will be for you to create a strong financial and investment plan that will support your goals. Remember, you can always change your investments in the long run if you find that they are no longer working in the way you want them to be, or if they don't serve you in the way you need.

Make sure that whenever you are investing your money that you are in it for the long haul. Investing for a short time frame is virtually pointless and will end up costing large amounts of money for you if you aren't careful. You need to have your long-term financial plan set up, even though it will likely change between now and then. You can always change it in the future if you need to. For shorter term savings needs, consider investing in something that is easy to liquefy, like a savings account or even a high-interest savings account.

Valuation Always Matters

When you are investing in a company or in stocks, you absolutely have to consider the valuation and the go from there. If you are not careful, you may end up paying large amounts or losing large amounts from this. The best way to start understanding how much you want to invest is using a bottom-up approach. How much is the company or stock valuated at? What is the history of the company or the stock? What is this specific company's promise? It is not uncommon for people to become blinded by the industry valuation itself and fail to recognize that the company holds its own unique valuation separate from the industry.

By using this bottom up approach you will be able to discover exactly what stocks are best for you to invest in and you will maximize your ability to get a strong return. Remember, just because a specific industry is striving doesn't mean that this individual business is thriving. It is best to put your money into good stock at a reasonable price, as this has a higher potential for you to earn. However, if you put your money into reasonable stock at a good price, you run a higher risk of losing out on a lot of returns. It is best to pay more for higher quality than it is to pay less for lower quality is ultimately what it comes down to. If you want to earn money, you are going to need to spend money. Invest in something with higher potential, instead of something with lower potential, and you will increase your likelihood of gaining a strong rate of return on your investment.

Pay Attention to the Real Rate of Return

When you are investing, there is an ideal rate of return that can be estimated based on the current stock market conditions and what is expected to happen. However, an estimation and an exact situation are two completely different things. It is important that you pay attention to the real rate of return on your investment, and take the time to understand this and keep it in mind. Doing this will help ensure that you make the right investment moves at the right time, and will prevent you from getting stuck in an idealistic mentality that could cost you lots of money. There are certain investments you can make that have a better guarantee and that come at lower costs, but ultimately most investments carry risk and you need to make sure that they are actually protecting you from inflation and maintaining your purchasing power.

Spread Your Risk Around (Diversify)

It has been stressed throughout this book that you need to really focus on diversifying your portfolio, and that is for good reason. Diversifying your portfolio reduces your risk and increases your potential. It does that by ensuring that if one area of your investments is not performing well, the rest will be protected from this situation. As well, if you are invested in several things then you have a higher potential of being involved in investments that will be doing well. It is the best way to increase your potential and decrease your risk when it comes to making investments.

Diversified portfolios are something that is recommended and encouraged in the investment industry. If you are working with an advisor, they are going to tell you to make sure that you are investing in a diversified portfolio for this very reason. The more you diversify, the better your chances are at having a greater return. It is basically a way of ensuring that you don't put all of your eggs in one basket.

Many people believe that diversify merely means buy several amounts of stock from a variety of different companies. This is actually not the case. You want to make sure that you invest in several different types of investments so that you get the best returns from your money. You should consider what your investment needs are and then invest in various different investment vehicles based on your needs. For example, you may wish to invest in a 401(k) for your retirement, a 529 prepaid tuition fee for your child's education, the stock market, a REIT, and any other number of investment styles. Doing this helps you diversify your portfolio in a way that protects your investments and ensures that you have the highest chance of earning a great return in one way or another.

Make Sure You Don't Go with The Flow

Earlier in this book, you were advised to ignore the media when you are invested in anything relating to the stock markets. This is for good reason: when you make decisions based on the media or the "general flow" you end up not making as much as you could. This is because you end up buying when the market is inflated and selling when the market is deflated. In order to make the promising gains that people always boast about when they talk about the stock markets, you are going to want to do the reverse and buy low and then sell high. That being said, when the media is crying out that stocks are on a downward spiral, you will actually want to buy more *not* sell more.

When people hear that the stock market is "crashing" their immediate instinct is to sell off their stock so that they don't suffer tremendous losses. What ends up happening, though, is that they destroy their rate of return. They don't realize that if they were to ride out the crash, or better yet, buy up a bunch of stocks during the crash, they would end up making a lot more money. If you look at a lengthy history of the stock market, it *always* bounces back after a crash. In fact, it generally bounces back better and stronger than it was before the crash. Knowing that, you can understand why it is important to endure these crashes and ride them out. Then, when the stock market is inflated again, you can sell off your stocks.

Many people get caught up with the media's influence and tend to make decisions based on the influence and end up missing out on large gains. It is very easy to do, especially considering that the media likes to hype everything up and exaggerate it, which can lead to a great fear among those who are invested. After all, there is always a risk that you could lose it all, so having someone tell you that you probably will is scary! The reality is, though, that the media often is just exaggerating and if you can ride it out, you will come back just fine and often stronger than you were when the market crashed.

To keep yourself from being one of the many that lose out on money this way, make sure that you *don't* go with the flow. Instead, do the opposite. When the market is crashing, buy up as much as you can. Then, when the market inflates again, you can sell off a bunch and generally earn a great profit back. This is the best way to make sure that you are getting back the maximum gains from your investments and that you set yourself up for monetary success in the future.

Only Invest in What You Understand
It can be easy to want to invest in anything that sounds good, but that is where it can get tricky and worrisome. If you are investing in something

that you don't understand, there are several things that can go wrong. First, you can end up investing in something that doesn't serve your needs properly. Or, you could end up investing in something that actually takes away from or deviates you away from your financial goals. It is important that you don't do this, especially if you want to stay on track.

A common mistake people make is that they gain a brief insight on what each investment style is and then they jump "all-in" and end up losing a lot of money. If you are looking to invest, a good idea is to make sure that you invest in something that you know about. This book is a great guide to help you get started, but another good idea is to get yourself an advisor who can further explain your desired investments in detail. A good investor *will* make sure that they educate you on everything that you are preparing to invest in, because knowing what you are investing in is the best way to ensure that it truly is a good fit for you. Remember, an advisor is just that: someone who gives advice. In the end, only you know what you need from your investments and therefore you have the final say. It is common for people to get themselves an advisor and then take them for their word. Later, they realize that they have made some unwise investments that have ended up costing them money in the long run. This is obviously the opposite of what you want to happen when you are investing. Knowing that, you should make sure that when you are working with an advisor you always pick someone who is more than willing to explain everything to you in a way that you understand. Those who make you feel as though they have it "all handled" are ones that you should be weary of. These individuals may not be working with all of your best interests in mind, as upsetting as that may be.

A good idea when you are preparing to invest is to take a browse through this book and consider your needs. Then, based on that, you should look at various vehicles that will help you meet those needs, and discover which ones have the best potential to fulfill your needs. Then, and only then, you should move forward with said investments. You may wish to hire someone to help you make these investments, or you may feel comfortable enough dealing with them on your own. Either way, make sure you are fully educated *before* you invest your money into anything. This could potentially save you from major losses.

Make Sure That You Avoid Complacency

There are many ways that you may become complacent in your investments, but it is absolutely vital that you avoid this at all costs. Complacency is what can end up costing you in large amounts and potentially losing you large amounts as well. The best thing that you can do is make sure that you take all of what you learn here and apply it to the best of your possible ability. You want to make sure that you are fully educated on the investments you are making, that you are monitoring their real rate of return, and that you are paying attention to what is going on with your money to ensure that it really is doing its work for you.

If you are investing money, you need to remember these common areas:
- Thoroughly understand your needs and goals
- Educate yourself on your options and their benefits, as well as their drawbacks
- Make an educated decision based on your needs and your investment personality
- Monitor your investments to ensure that they are performing well

Another thing you need to do is avoid basing your investments on past performances. Many times people think "well, this stock has been performing well so I think it will perform well again in the future". There are three things you need to consider when you are saying this: 1) how is it performing *right now?* 2) How is the company/stock performing overall and what is an honest outlook for them? 3) What is the outlook for the industry? By honestly addressing these questions and taking them into consideration, you can make an educated guess that will help ensure that you will be more likely to gain back your money plus a healthy rate of return.

Many people get complacent when they are investing and they fail to realize how crucial it is to make smart decisions. The idea that "I have plenty of time to gain it back" often comes into play and has people failing to realize that wasted time is lost time and that the same goes for money. If you can prevent yourself from entering an uneducated risk that could end up losing large amounts of money, obviously that is the better route to go. You can avoid this by avoiding complacency altogether.

If You Don't Know, Ask

There is a reason why there are so many brokerages and investment advisers. It can be hard to know where to start and what to do! As someone who is new and likely uneducated in this sector, it can be hard to get yourself started in investing and ensure that you are doing the smartest thing with your money. It is important that if you are unsure or if you have questions that you ask. There is nothing wrong with hiring a brokerage to help you make sure that you are getting the best out of your money. In fact, it's encouraged! The more you can educate yourself and make smart decisions with your money, the better the chance will be that you make a great rate of return on it.

Investing money can be a hard thing to do, especially with all of the different investment vehicles available to you. When you are investing, you should never feel shy to ask questions from people who know what they are doing. You want to ensure that you are asking the right person by making sure that they have your best interest in mind. But, once you have found the right person, you should never hesitate to ask them any questions that you may have. That's what they're there for, after all.

Be Realistic About Your Risk Tolerance

Many people see the promise of "higher return potential" and fail to realize the "higher risk potential" associated with it. Or, equally as bad, they see the "lower risk potential" and fail to realize that it also comes with a "lower return potential" attached to it. These optimistic or fearful outlooks on investments can actually end up costing you a lot of money if you aren't careful. There are smart times to expose yourself to higher risk and there are smart times to expose yourself to lower rates of returns. There are many things that go into play for this, as you have learned throughout this book. In case you have forgotten, here is what you need to remember:

- Your risk should be balanced out with the length of your investment, as in:
- A shorter investment term should be attached with a lower risk rating. And,
- A longer investment term should be attached with a higher risk rating.

Despite knowing that balance, you also want to consider what you are comfortable with. If you are comfortable going a little higher with your risk on a short-term investment because you know it isn't as important to you if you endure a loss, then you are the one who will know that answer. If you aren't as comfortable enduring higher losses on a longer-term investment because the money means a lot to you and you don't want to risk it, then listen to your instinct. Generally speaking, though, your investment risk tolerance should be balanced out with the length of your investment and how much you need that money, as well as when. Balancing your investments properly will help ensure that you are earning the best possible return based on your needs surrounding your investment.

Reinvest

When you are making money on your investments, you should always consider reinvesting the return you make on your investments. This will help ensure that you are making the maximum income from your investments. When you reinvest the money you make from your investments, you increase your principle and therefore increase the return rate that you will earn on your investments. This is a powerful way to rapidly increase your investment and make even more off of it. If you speak with any reputable adviser, they will almost always recommend that you reinvest your return to maximize your overall return from that particular investment.

There are many rules you should focus on when you are investing money. It is not something that you should take lightly, as you work hard for your money and you want to make sure that your money is working hard for you in return. People use investing as an opportunity to secure their future, and because of that you are going to want to make sure that you invest smartly so that your future is secured and protected. While you will learn more as you go, these basic rules are things that you need to consider to ensure that you are keeping your investments protected and that you are making as much back as possible.

When you are starting out, it can be hard and overwhelming. You may not know exactly what to invest or how. The best thing you can do is focus on these rules and the other things you have learned in this book. If you are still unsure about what to do, you can always go ahead and get yourself a financial adviser who will be able to further educate you on your options and make sure that you are getting the best from your investments. Remember, advisers are people who have gained an education specifically in investing, so they will be able to help you solidify your plan and invest your money in the best way possible. As long as you ensure that you have a knowledgeable and reputable adviser, you will be fine.

Conclusion

Investing your money may seem intimidating, but it is important that you do it. In this day and age, it is vital that you are investing in your future. Doing this protects you from inflation, wage losses, and other expected and unexpected changes that can have a negative impact on your money if you are not careful. Investing used to be something that only the wealthy did, but nowadays it is important that everyone does this. Whether you are an individual, a non-profit, or a business owner, you need to be knowledgeable in the world of investing and what it can do for you.

At first, it may seem overwhelming as there are a lot of things for you to consider.

The best way for you to start is to simply create a plan of what your needs are. Think about everything that you know that you will need in the future and write it all down. From there, you can start researching the options available to you so that you can invest in your needs and make sure that you are making the right moves that will maximize your rate of return.

If you are struggling with getting started, or if you are worrying that you won't make the right decisions, the best thing that you can do is get yourself a financial adviser. This individual should be someone who is reputable and knowledgeable and who will help educate you on your options and everything that your money can do to serve you now and in the future. Once you find an adviser that works for you, you can work together with them to make sure that you make the best moves to invest your money in a way that is smart for you.

I hope that reading this book helped you create a powerful financial plan that will set you up for success both now and in your future for all of your desires. Having a strong plan is the best way to ensure that you set yourself up well for any unexpected situations, or for expected situations such as education funds or retirement. Talking about investments can be boring, especially if you don't understand them, but they really are a critical part of life these days.

The next step, if you haven't already, is to start creating your financial plan. Remember that you need to consider everything: your retirement, any major investments you want to make, and protecting yourself from unexpected situations such as wage losses or critical illnesses. Once you have created this plan, you should start researching which investment vehicles are going to be able to serve your needs in the best way possible. Then, you can go ahead and start building your portfolio! You want to make sure that you are investing with the right risk tolerance and in the right investment vehicles to ensure that you are securing and protecting your future self. Doing this will arrange for you to be set up with financial freedom, which is an incredibly important thing to do.

Lastly, if you enjoyed this book, I ask that you please take the time to rate it and leave your review on Amazon. Your honest opinion and feedback would be greatly appreciated!

Thank you again for purchasing *Investing for Beginners: An Introduction to Easy and Successful Investing*. I hope this book has served you well and I wish you luck in your investment journey!

www.ingramcontent.com/pod-product-compliance
Lightning Source LLC
Chambersburg PA
CBHW070046210526
45170CB00012B/602